From
PROGNOSIS
To
PEACE

TRIGGER™
Your Specialist Mental Health & Wellbeing Hub

From PROGNOSIS To PEACE

NAVIGATING *Grief* THROUGH
Discovery, Gratitude AND *Healing*

LARA RODWELL

First published in Great Britain 2021 by Cherish Editions
Cherish Editions is a trading style of Shaw Callaghan Ltd
& Shaw Callaghan 23 USA, INC.

The Foundation Centre
Navigation House, 48 Millgate, Newark
Nottinghamshire NG24 4TS UK

www.triggerhub.org

British Library Cataloguing in Publication Data
A CIP catalogue record for this book is available upon request
from the British Library

ISBN: 978-1-913615-31-4

This book is also available in the following eBook formats:
ePUB: 978-1-913615-32-1

Cherish Editions encourages diversity and different viewpoints. However, all views, thoughts and opinions expressed in this book are the author's own and are not necessarily representative of us as an organisation. All material in this book is set out in good faith for general guidance and no liability can be accepted for loss or expense incurred in following the information given. In particular this book is not intended to replace expert medical or psychiatric advice. It is intended for informational purposes only and for your own personal use and guidance. It is not intended to act as a substitute for professional medical advice. The author is not a medical practitioner nor a counsellor, and professional advice should be sought if desired before embarking on any health related programme.

Introduction

Letter to the reader

Dear friend,

I'd like to begin with a heartfelt apology. I am truly sorry that your circumstances have led to you being here. I wish things could be different for you and your loved one. Wherever you are on your journey with grief, the spectrum of emotions you could be feeling right now may seem utterly overwhelming. If this is the case, take a deep breath in, then out. Don't push yourself to continue if you don't feel ready.

If you've received this as a gift, be gentle with yourself as you explore what this journal can offer you. If you've bought this for yourself, be proud of the strength you've found to initiate your healing journey during this extremely difficult time.

I embody the waves of grief myself, daily. In March 2020, my dad was given a six-month prognosis, after being diagnosed with an aggressive form of bowel cancer. It was around the same time of the first Covid-induced British lockdown, which blessed my family with two silver linings: time and togetherness. The six of us spent the summer months of 2020 talking, writing, laughing and reminiscing. We were grateful for every single moment and felt privileged that we had the opportunity to create those memories together.

On the morning of 5th September 2020, in the care of our local hospice, my dad died. His physical body left this earth and it was over, just like that.

Those six months felt like a gift. A gift of time and wisdom. I was granted the opportunity to gain a new perspective on my own relationship with life, as Dad neared the end of his. Others aren't so lucky.

For once, I wasn't trying to control the uncontrollable – longing to fix, understand or problem solve. Instead of resisting a situation that was completely out of my hands, I trusted that the universe had dealt my family these cards for a reason. I believed, one day, that reason would make sense to me. At the time, all I could do was be present, with my Dad, for as long as I possibly could.

Each of the following chapters includes extracts from the journal I shared with my dad and insights I've gained from them. It's difficult to be vulnerable, I know, but I hope my sharing will inspire you to open your heart and let your feelings be seen.

I'd be lying if I told you that the shadow of grief doesn't haunt me, or if I said there aren't days where I feel helpless and numb. What I can tell you, though, is that there *is* hope.

There is hope for a future brighter than you could ever imagine.

For a sense of purpose that will embody every cell of your being.

And for an inner glow that will bring you deep comfort, healing and peace.

Now, I imagine you're asking yourself several questions. Is this journal right for me? What benefit does it have? How do I use it? Your time is precious now, more than ever. You need to be especially conscious of what you put your time and energy into. So, before we begin, I want you to be sure that this journal will benefit *your* journey from prognosis to peace.

Does this journal speak to me?

If you've picked this up, you might feel like everyone around you is tiptoeing around the fact that you're dying. Or you might have things you want to say to a loved one, but worry the conversation might be too uncomfortable to out loud. Perhaps you're longing for something physical to keep your loved one's memory alive.

Whoever you are, wherever you come from, you're not alone. I know you must feel lost and disorientated, like your whole world has been flipped upside down. I understand how desperate you must feel to wake up from this nightmare. You might be feeling angry and confused, asking yourself, "Why me?" and "Why our family?". Whatever you're feeling, it's okay. We're going to get through this together.

As hard as it is to acknowledge, death is an unspoken truth that impacts every single one of our lives. Nevertheless, as a society we tend to distract, avoid or veer away from the topic, which only makes it harder when you or someone you love receives a terminal prognosis. I know how you feel. For me, this was an isolating, confusing and frustrating place to find myself.

What benefit does it have?

From Prognosis to Peace bridges a difficult, but vital gap in communication. It grants you permission to gently start your grieving process with your loved one, before fate takes its toll. I know from first-hand experience that this is not easy. In fact, accepting the fact my dad was going to die was probably the hardest thing I've ever done or ever will do. However, the peace I felt once I could talk about it with him was an invaluable part of my healing journey. I'm here to meet you where you're at, right now, and guide you from a place of empathy and compassion. By the end of it, I hope you will feel stronger, lighter and more connected to yourself, your loved one and the world around you.

How do I use it?

This journal is split into five sections, which you can work through in any order you wish. I encourage you to respond to how you're feeling in the moment, turning to the page that speaks to you at any given time.

To help you do so, I have three simple tips for filling in this journal:

1. **You do you.** Don't feel like you need to fill in the sections, chapters or prompts consecutively. This isn't a revision guide; it won't be marked.

2. **Go easy on yourself.** Don't force yourself to write every day. This isn't a daily diary, but a space to record personal reflections and insights.

INTRODUCTION

3. **Take your time.** Don't feel guilty if you can't bring yourself to
    open the journal for days or even weeks – this is not homework,
    it's healing.

If you wish to reflect on an observation or event, write a letter in
Section Three. If you have memories you want to share, fill in a
journal prompt in Section One or Two. If you find a stash of photos
in the bottom of your wardrobe, pick your favourites and create a
collage in Section Four. There is no rhyme or reason to this journal.
There is no 'right' way to fill it in. Remember that this is yours and
theirs – no one else's.

With love,

Lara x

> *"Trauma creates change you don't choose.*
> *Healing is about creating change*
> *you do choose."*

MICHELE ROSENTHAL

Practice 1: The
Impermanence Inventory

Take five minutes, each day, to contemplate the
impermanent nature of all aspects of your life:
your relationships, objects, people, emotions and
situations.

Softly say to yourself, "All things have a beginning
and an end. I have a beginning and an end. I am
part of nature, always changing, and one day
this body will dissolve into the infinite stream of
consciousness. I accept the impermanence of life,
and in doing so, I am free from fear and anxiety."

Thoughts from the author: Mindfulness routines have been a regular part of my daily life since I was a teenager. However, they were especially important to me after Dad received his prognosis. Reminding myself of the impermanence of life shifted my perspective on the nature of change. From the seasons to our feelings, to our circumstances – everything around us, and within us – is always changing. I began to accept that change is the only certainty in life, so resisting the future or dwelling on the past is, ultimately, pointless. By taking a few minutes out of my day to do short practices like this one, I gradually opened myself up to the idea of making lemonade out of life's sourest lemon. By focusing solely on living in the present, slowly and steadily, one day at a time, I started to move towards a stronger sense of peace.

Section One

LISTS FOR YOU

Chapter One

Top Fives

YOUR TOP FIVE MEMORIES:

YOUR TOP FIVE SONGS:

YOUR TOP FIVE PLACES TO VISIT:

YOUR TOP FIVE FILMS:

YOUR TOP FIVE BOOKS:

Nothing and no one can take away all those great memories from us. It's one of the reasons why I do feel some peace in the current situation. I am lucky to have shared those experiences with you and although we have also shared some really hard times over the last few years, getting through the bad times seems to make the good memories appear better."

David Rodwell, 17 April 2020

Thoughts: Dad enjoyed filling in these lists the most (he often broke the five-per-list instructions – typical!). For me, they were the most useful and practical at the time of his prognosis. From there on out, I had quick access to specific things he valued and loved. Together, we reminisced over the memories, made a playlist of the songs, visited as many of the places as we could (we couldn't quite make it as far as the Caribbean, unfortunately!), watched all the movies and reread all the books. Relieving these simple experiences was, in a way, his bucket list.

Chapter Two

Your Favourite Five

YOUR FAVOURITE QUOTE:

YOUR FAVOURITE FOOD:

YOUR FAVOURITE PLACE TO RELAX:

YOUR FAVOURITE SEASON:

YOUR FAVOURITE TIME OF YEAR:

"When your fear touches someone's pain, it becomes pity. When your love touches someone's pain, it becomes compassion."

STEPHEN LEVINE

Thoughts from the author: Dad's positivity, the daily practices I put in place, and the support of my friends and family inspired me to respond to the prognosis with love and positivity for a life well lived; not fear and despair for the suffering that was taking place. It was important for me to focus on the good, as much as I could. Noting his favourite everyday experiences not only provided light-hearted comfort for my dad in the moment, but also inspired traditions and ways to celebrate his legacy in the years to come.

Chapter Three

Your Wisdom

YOUR ONE PIECE OF ADVICE:

YOUR MOST MEANINGFUL LIFE LESSON:

YOUR BIGGEST MISTAKE:

YOUR GREATEST ACHIEVEMENT:

YOUR GREATEST FEAR:

"*I know I'm weak on the outside, but on the inside I feel strong. It's not just about me though, it's about you guys. Mum, you four kids, we're a collective power with no particular purpose other than to be and not leave anyone behind. We've been dealt a pack of cards and chosen to play them to our advantage. Honestly, I look at what has happened here and although I would've liked the future to be different, as a family I don't think we would've ever had this meaningful time together if it wasn't for this.*"

– David Rodwell, 20 May 2020

Thoughts from the author: Getting a deeper insight into Dad's perception of this time together, and the wisdom he embodied, provided me with the tools to navigate my grief moving forward. These introspective lists gave him the opportunity to contemplate what he's learnt from his time on this earth, feel empowered by what he's achieved and consider what he can pass onto the lives of others.

Practice 2: Digital Reminders

I'm not sure if you're familiar with the voice memo widget on your smartphone – I wasn't before this. However, during those six months, it became my best friend. I began to (discreetly) record conversations my dad and I had that I sensed would be particularly insightful in the future. This was especially important as I noticed the tone of Dad's voice start to change. It became lighter. Slower. He spoke with more ease. As time goes by, I know the sound of his voice – his storytelling, his wisdom, his laughter – will bring me a huge sense of comfort.

35

Section Two

LISTS FOR ME

Chapter Four

Gratitude

THE MOST SIGNIFICANT LESSON YOU'VE TAUGHT ME:

THE REASONS WHY I'M PROUD OF YOU:

THE IMPACT YOU'VE HAD ON MY LIFE SO FAR:

THE IMPACT YOU'LL HAVE ON MY FUTURE:

THE LESSON I WILL SHARE WITH OTHERS:

*"Be grateful for your life, every detail of it,
and your face will come to shine like a sun,
and everyone who sees it will be made
glad and peaceful."*

RUMI

Practice 3: Daily Gratitude

My dad was a humble man and greatly underestimated the impact he had on the lives of others, all throughout his life. As well as these lists, I texted him every evening with something I was grateful to him for. This is another practice you can incorporate into your day-to-day life if it strikes you as meaningful. Daily gratitude was, and still is, a fundamental part of my healing journey.

Three Hats

Three hats by 2pm,

The man who does it all.

A dad, a carpenter, a wonderful husband,

He ain't nobody else's fool.

Nothing's too much for this man who awakes,

At 5am every day.

He'll have built a table by breakfast time,

And fixed the roof by midday.

Did I mention he's also a maths teacher?

He gave O'Kang a run for his money.

Also, a lawyer that writes savage contracts,

And a guitarist whose performances are funny.

He waters the neighbour's plants,

And defends the needy in court.

There's nothing this man can't do,

And nothing he cannot sort.

To him we're forever grateful,

For everything he's ever done.

Three hats by 2pm,

His efforts are second to none.

Lara Rodwell, 21 April 2020

Chapter Five

Memories

WHAT I WILL MISS ABOUT YOU THE MOST:

WHAT WILL REMIND ME OF YOU:

WHAT I WILL REMEMBER ABOUT THIS TIME:

WHAT I WILL REMIND MYSELF OF WHEN I'M STRUGGLING:

WHAT I HAVE LEARNT ABOUT US:

SECTION 2: *Lists for Me*

*"What we have once enjoyed deeply
we can never lose. All that we love deeply
becomes a part of us."*

HELEN KELLER

Thoughts from the author: Reflecting on the profoundness of this time together as a family was important to both of us. We often talked about the likelihood of people outside the family pitying us, but pity is the last thing we felt for ourselves. In fact, quite the opposite, as we often described feeling like the 'luckiest family in the world'. The preciousness of this time woke us up to the revelation that it's the love and joy we share with each other that makes a life complete.

This Time

Every moment of gratitude,

Every single second of peace.

I'll never forget this time together,

The nostalgia will forever run deep.

We've laughed, cried, and talked a lot,

No subject we have not covered.

You know every single one of my dreams,

My thoughts and ideas you've discovered.

To be part of this loving family,

Means taking the good with the bad.

No experience that we will not learn from,

No life that will be lived, sad.

This is the hardest blow of them all,

But together we'll break through the grief.

These moments will always be in our hearts,

For time is our only thief.

Lara Rodwell, 30 June 2020

Chapter Six

My Life

My biggest dream:

My strongest values:

My goal for this time next year:

My biggest fear for the future:

My favourite quote:

*"Ignoring death leaves us with a false
sense of life's permanence and perhaps
encourages us to lose ourselves in the minutiae
of daily life. Obsessive rumination on death,
on the other hand, can lead us away from life.
Honestly coming to terms with one's death
involves reflection on its significance in one's life
and thinking about the larger values that give
life its meaning. In the end, it is useful
to think about death only to the point that it
frees us to live fully immersed in the life we
have yet to live."*

JEFF MASON

Thoughts: Dad's sudden prognosis opened my eyes to the finality of my physical existence on this earth. It shined a light on my values, priorities and what was holding me back from living to my full potential. Consciously acknowledging the mortality of my own being deepened my appreciation of life going forward. I wanted Dad to know that I wasn't just going to accept his prognosis, but I was going to use it as an opportunity to live a more meaningful life. I felt comforted by the belief that he would be watching over me and that one day we'd all be together again. This brought even more lightness, humour and ease into those last few months.

The Family in the Stars

One day we'll be together again,

The family in the stars.

Dad is the first to make his way up,

I hope he checks out all the good bars!

He'll always be with us in spirit,

At every event we'll leave him a seat.

But for now, he's dying for a lamb madras,

And a beer or two to soften the heat.

My god, you'll love his dance moves up there,

SECTION 2: *Lists for Me*

He'll give Freddie a run for his money.

His accents will entertain the masses, I'm sure,

The 'American schoolgirl' is particularly funny!

Don't let him worry about us too much,

We'll be sure to behave down here.

Our six stars will shine together one day,

In my heart that's nothing but clear.

Lara Rodwell, 5 August 2020

Section Three

SPACE FOR US

"I do not fear death. I had been dead for billions and billions of years before I was born, and had not suffered the slightest inconvenience from it."

MARK TWAIN

Thoughts from the author: In our letters and poems to each other, we discussed a vast range of topics – from the TV shows we were watching (our joint favourite was *Alaska: The Last Frontier*), Covid-19 and weird dreams we were experiencing, all the way to the side effects of chemotherapy. Together with the lists, we covered a lot of ground in a short space of time. Writing became a creative way to communicate and express our inner worlds. Soon enough, our imaginations went wild. With a shared (rather dark) sense of humour, we decided to name Dad's tumour 'Tod' – the new family scapegoat.

We tried not to take life too seriously and became expert at bringing silliness and laughter into any moment, especially as Dad's condition got worse. In fact, I think I laughed more during 2020 than I have in any other year of my life. Absolutely absurd.

Tod & Covid ('Brothers in Harms')

We named my Tumour Tod,

On account of he's a sod.

Who thinks it's cool,

Messing up my stool,

Sod off 'cos you ain't no God.

And as for Viral Covid,

Bro, on it put a lid,

And keep it there,

'Til vaccines here,

And of you we are rid.

David Rodwell, 19 April 2020

SECTION 3: *Space For Us*

SECTION 3: *Space For Us*

Section Four

MEMORIES WE SHARE

"And when great souls die, after a period,
peace blooms – slowly and always irregularly.
Spaces fill with a kind of soothing electric
vibration. Our senses, restored, never to be the
same, whisper to us. They existed.
They existed. We can be. Be and be better.
For they existed."

MAYA ANGELOU

Thoughts: One of the first things that sprung to my (overly sentimental) mind when Dad received his prognosis was the thought of him not being at my, entirely hypothetical and probably now jinxed, wedding. In that moment, I genuinely recall feeling like the ground was caving away underneath me, like my life may as well be over. So, after a three-hour meltdown, do you know what I did? I asked him to write me a wedding speech (which he left in his will in due course).

So, why the sob story? Well, grief is the time for you and your loved one to be selfish. Hear me out. Selfishness is a character trait I don't, fortunately, tend to exhibit very often (another genetic predisposition, thanks Dad). However, I had a personal revelation that if there was any time or reason to be selfish, it's now.

Selfish with the support you require from family and friends, as well as the boundaries you set in terms of your personal space or privacy. *Continues overleaf...*

Selfish with the way you treat and comfort yourself –
always putting your health first, no matter what.

Selfish with what you need from your loved one, if it's
going to help you feel more at peace.

Whether it's a letter, an item of clothing or a book that
they've had since childhood, ask for it. The worst they can
do is say no. You know the memories you have of them
will never be forgotten, but you're only human. We all
get attached to ideas and objects and experiences (even
hypothetical ones we haven't had yet!). Don't be afraid to
ask for what you need.

A Celebration

I will go through this life living for you,

For your time has been cut short.

No risk I won't take or person I won't meet,

No opportunity I will abort.

Every choice I make I'll turn to you,

Trusting your glimmer will shine through me.

For there won't be a single day that goes by,

Where your memory won't set me free.

My life is going to be a celebration,

As I've got nothing left to lose,

I'll 'Lara dance' to my heart's content,

And dedicate every toast to you.

You raised me to be resilient,

'Small but mighty' through every storm.

You made me believe I could do anything,

My rock from the moment I was born.

Sure, there'll be times when I'm overwhelmed,

Not sure who to turn to or who to be.

But in those times, I'll look for a sign,

A sign that you're sending a message to me.

I know you'll look down from time to time,

So rest assured, I will behave.

You won't be short of a good people-watch,

With our four entertaining ways.

Your life has touched so many hearts,

It makes me so unbelievably proud.

You've inspired me to reach for my dreams,

To be brave, bold, and loud.

In my children's eyes, I will see you,

Through their smiles, I'll hear your laugh.

Your legacy will be treasured forever,

No memory of you that won't last.

You truly are my greatest role model,

My adventure buddy through and through.

You're not only my past but my future,

This, I hope you already knew.

Lara Rodwell, 14 June 2020

SECTION 4: *Memories We Share*

SECTION 4: *Memories We Share*

Section Five

AFTER YOU'VE GONE

Chapter Seven

Discovery

WHAT HAVE I LEARNT FROM THIS EXPERIENCE?

WHAT ARE MY NEW BELIEFS?

WHAT HAS IMPROVED IN MY LIFE?

WHAT IS HOLDING ME BACK?

WHAT WOULD THEY SAY TO ME RIGHT NOW?

"Grief can be the garden of compassion.
If you keep your heart open through everything,
your pain can become your greatest ally in your
life's search for love and wisdom."

RUMI

Thoughts from the author: My dad dying was a wake-up call for me. It shifted my perspective on, well, everything. I'd always been opportunistic, adventurous and open-minded, and I'd always worked hard for what I wanted. However, what hadn't quite clicked was the power I had within me to let go of what I *didn't* want. The self-critical thoughts. The toxic friendships. The attachments that didn't serve me. All that baggage is useless in the face of a death sentence.

The plot twist comes when we truly appreciate the reality of our existence: *that we're ALL facing a death sentence, and not one of us is exempt.*

So, why are we beating ourselves up all the time? Judging others for just being themselves? Holding back our truths out of fear? Striving to be someone we're not? Living out someone else's dream? If we're all facing a death sentence, *surely* that's a reason to not waste a second listening to our head and not our heart.

The Whole

Going through life more gently now,

Less pressure and less to do.

Allowing my body to simply 'be',

Starting this chapter anew.

To be with 'what is' – the good and the bad,

Letting go the need to control.

Accepting of life's uncertainty,

Knowing it's all just part of the whole.

Taking the knocks within my stride,

As we're all doing the best we can.

No one of us has done this before,

This, the universe had planned.

As beings we're in this together,

So, what's war and constant strife?

For if all of us just have one chance,

Let's not waste this sacred life.

Lara Rodwell, 12 January 2021

Chapter Eight

Healing

How could I bring more compassion into my life?

How could I use this experience to help others?

How has this experience helped me grow?

How can I show up more for others?

How has my relationship with the world changed?

"You only live in the present, this fleeting moment. The rest of your life is already gone or not yet revealed."

MARCUS AURELIUS

Thoughts from the author: As a family, how we respond to the world around us has changed in subtle ways since Dad died. We look out for more things to be grateful for. We eat pointless dramas and semi-frustrations for breakfast on the daily. We see Dad as part of everything that surrounds us – a rainbow in the sky, a hovering bird and even the leaky sink (he always did enjoy pushing our buttons).

Whether you're spiritual or not, I believe that thinking of yourself as part of a bigger whole is the key to feeling more at peace with death – whether it's your own or someone else's. I count the lessons I've learnt through the heartache of grief and loss as bittersweet gifts. Alongside the hardship, I've gained perspective, clarity and a new level of presence – all of which I'll be eternally grateful for.

Everything

I said to you,

That you'd know everything,

And now you do.

The before and the after,

You are here and there.

Not limited.

Understanding the why and the where.

The here and the now,

Is where we are,

But where we've been and where we'll go,

You know that too.

Maggie Rodwell, 10 January 2021

SECTION 5: *After You've Gone*

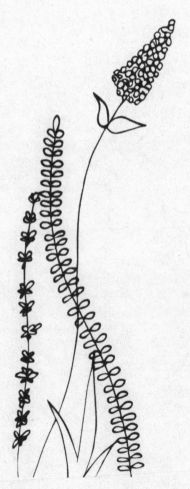

Chapter Nine

Now

TODAY, I AM FEELING:

TODAY, I FEEL PROUD OF MYSELF FOR:

TODAY, I NEED TO LET GO OF:

TODAY, I AM GRATEFUL FOR:

TODAY, I FEEL AT PEACE BECAUSE:

"Each night, the crickets sing of impermanence. Their songs remind us that whenever one thing ends, so another begins."

CRISTEN RODGERS

Thoughts from the author: My journey with grief isn't over and I'm not sure it ever will be. However, what I do know is that, through conscious awareness and effort, I *will* heal.

My greatest gift has been embracing wholeness. The wholeness of everything I am, every moment as it is and every person as they are. Each of us, perfectly imperfect, were put on this planet for a reason. That reason is unique for each of us – whoever we are, wherever we come from and whatever we choose to be.

Practice 4: Positive Impacts

Take a moment to reflect on one thing you've said or done that's had a positive impact on someone's life – a friend, a family member, a colleague or even a stranger. Close your eyes and visualize it now. How did it make you feel? Did you notice the effect this had on their life?

Now, reflect on a time someone said or did something that's had a positive impact on *your* life. How did you respond? Did you notice the effect they had on your life at the time?

Thoughts from the author: You can visualize the differences you make in life as pebbles being thrown in a lake. Every time you throw a pebble, you send ripples across the water further than the eye can see – deep within the streams, under the lily pads, among the reeds. Beyond all streams of consciousness and forms of life, your existence on this earth is part of something bigger and deeper than you could ever imagine. You're constantly sending ripples through your energy, love and presence. Our seemingly insignificant impact is connected to everything and everyone, even when we die. The energy of the love you share is infinite.

Believe in your reason to exist *and* your reason to die. Don't give up until you're living the life you want; a life you truly love – full of joy, happiness and ease. You're never too old to start anew, for the universe knows no age. You're never too broken to heal, for the universe will guide you to peace – if you let it. In the words of Hillel the Elder, "If not now, when?"

Notes from the Author

In my opinion, the most magical thing about this life is is that no-one experiences it the same. No matter how similar our upbringing, or genetics, we all see the world differently (even identical twins, as I've experienced first-hand!). Despite this, life-changing experiences can connect us, and shape our shared values, in ways like no other. Be it a global pandemic, the illness or death of a loved one, or something as seemingly trivial as England losing the Euros; as humans, we have the innate capacity to turn any adversity into an advantage. Together we can create communities – in person, virtually or purely through the energy we vibrate everyday – that tackle the pressing issue of feeling alone in a world where no-one sees the world in the same way that we do as individuals.

Death is one of those things that, as a culture, we tend to ignore until we're in the thick of it – whether it's ourselves or a loved one who is dying. Personally, I think this is irresponsible as, from an educational perspective, we should be taught about the realities that come with the fleeting and unpredictable nature of our existence from a young age – not just history, languages, and headache-inducing maths equations. This time last year, I couldn't comprehend how I'd cope with my dad dying at the age of 54 years old, let alone how to face the idea of my own morality. Yet, this is something we will all face in one form or another.

When dad received his prognosis, my mind felt absolutely frazzled. As a naturally optimistic and idealistic individual, I didn't think anything like this could happen to a man who seemed to deserve nothing but fun, love and happiness in life. I'd always been a strong believer that 'what goes around, comes around' – therefore, seeing my dad suffer to such an extent was the last thing I expected to witness. It was impossible for me to rationalize without earnestly accepting that there must be a reason behind such an unfortunate circumstance. I knew there had to be a silver lining to be uncovered and was confident the lesson to be learnt was greater than the tragedy of the life we were about to lose.

Over the next six months, the gift that was to come from the premature passing of my Dad's life was bubbling away deep down underneath the surface. The deterioration happened quickly, the suffering was difficult to watch, and the grief of losing his physical body was painful. Then, early one autumnal morning, a month after dad died, it hit me. As I wrestled with the grief that kept me awake each night, I turned a vague, and rather abstract concept, into something tangible. I suddenly knew what needed to be said, and the form in which I needed to say it. The seed of creating a guided grief journal, to accompany the victims and families of those facing a terminal prognosis, was planted.

From the moment I started writing this book, putting words onto paper was my source of therapy. Despite being surrounded by family and friends, who I knew would do anything to support me, I still felt lonely and alone. The elephant in the room, that my dad had just died in a rather disturbing and traumatic way, was a burden that I could no longer ignore or distract myself from through work, socializing, or future planning. I wanted to use the hardship that I faced to help others in a similar situation, and I felt the most appropriate way I could do this was through writing. Somehow, some way, I wanted to get what I'd learnt from my dad, in such a short space of time, out there for people to read. I intended to spread his ripples of wisdom, love, and gratitude into a world where people are suffering just like he did. I knew there was magic in the energy we shared, as a family, during those six months. If nothing else, I owed it to my dad's legacy to transform the insights he formed, towards the end of his life, into tools that could potentially help those facing a similar fate.

So, here I am now, ten months on, stronger than I've ever felt before. This book marks the tail-end of a short, but life-affirming, chapter of a journey that I wouldn't trade for the world. The strength I've gained from my dad's suffering was the wake-up call I needed to realize how precious our time on this earth is, and how important it is to make the most out of every single second.

My dad's response to adversity taught me that we all have the power within us to accept what we can't control with humility and appreciation for a life well lived. His unconditional love and unfathomable loyalty to his family demonstrated our collective ability to prioritize who, and what, is truly important in our lives – especially when sh*t hits the fan. His sense of humour, all the way through, inspired me to continue making others smile just like he made me, my family and everyone who had the privilege of meeting him. His journey, from prognosis to peace, was a magical one. Six months, not just of suffering, but of love, laughter, and life-changing insights. In the words of Irving Stone, "There is no love without pain." However, as my Dad so beautifully wrote, "Love's alive for evermore."

For now, friends, that's me. Happy, alive, and forever grateful for this opportunity to provide a space for others to feel more at ease in this world of uncertainty, pain, and loss.

Feel everything, appreciate everyone, and don't take life too seriously - it's way too short to waste, but way too long not to enjoy.

Lots of Love,

Lara x

NOTES FROM THE AUTHOR

119

Half a Year

Things have changed in half a year,

The illness, sadness, ready fear.

Arms and legs were stronger then,

But now are weak and wafer thin.

Nature has dealt a blow,

But does not on me alone bestow.

Its power, plunging in the knife,

Twisting, fuming, ending life.

Is suffered by us all sometime,

Young and old and small canine.

Then its awe starts out anew,

In flower, bird and morning dew.

NOTES FROM THE AUTHOR

In baby, puppy, kitten too,

Monkey, tree and Hopping Roo.

I see the wonder clearer now,

Just as well in view of how.

My time is running out of here,

And eye is running out of tear.

But all is good, of that I know,

Love lives on in all to show.

And through my kids I see for sure,

That love's alive for evermore.

David Rodwell, 6 June 2020

BIBLIOGRAPHY

Books

Brazier, J, *The Grief Survival Guide: How to Navigate Loss and All That Comes With It*, Hodder & Stoughton, London, 2017

Coelho, P, *Eleven Minutes:* HarperOne, San Francisco, CA, 2005

Essbaum, J.A, *The Good Grief Journal: A Journey toward Healing*, Fortress Press, Minneapolis, MN, 2019

Hill, J, *Locke & Key Volume 6: Alpha & Omega*, IDW Publishing, San Diego, CA, 2014

Keller, H, *We Bereaved*, Isha Books, Delhi, 2013

Klein, A, *Embracing Life After Loss: A Gentle Guide for Growing through Grief.* Mango, Miami, FL, 2019

Owen, K, *Life, Without You: A Journal through Grief*, Ultimate Publications, Liverpool, 2018

Pigliucci, M, *How to Be a Stoic: Using Ancient Philosophy to Live a Modern Life*, Basic Books, New York, 2017

Samuel, J, *Grief Works: Stories of Life, Death and Surviving.* Penguin Life, London, 2018

Seneca, *Dialogues and Letters*, Penguin Classics, London, 1997

Willis, C B & Crawford Samuelson, M, *Opening to Grief: Finding Your Way from Loss to Peace*, Dharma Spring, Newburyport, MA, 2020

[B] **Journals**

Gilhooly, M L M & Sweeting, H N, 'Anticipatory Grief: A Review', *Social Science & Medicine, 30*(10), 1073-1080, 1990

Johansson, A K & Grimby, A, 'Anticipatory Grief Among Close Relatives of Patients in Hospice and Palliative Wards', *American Journal of Hospice and Palliative Medicine*, 2011

Kissane, D W; Bloch, S; McKenzie, D P; McKenzie, M; Moskowitz, C; O'Neill, I, 'Family Focused Grief Therapy: A Randomized, Controlled Trial in Palliative Care and Bereavement', *The American Journal of Psychiatry*, 2006

Maciejewski, P K & Prigerson, H G, 'Grief and acceptance as opposite sides of the same coin: setting a research agenda to study peaceful acceptance of loss', *The British Journal of Psychiatry*, 2018

Simon, N M, 'Treating Complicated Grief', *The Journal of the American Medical Association*, 2013

Online

#griefjourney, *Instagram*, 2020
https://www.instagram.com/explore/tags/griefjourney/
#griefrecovery, *Instagram*, 2020
https://www.instagram.com/explore/tags/griefrecovery/
#healing, *Instagram*, 2020
https://www.instagram.com/explore/tags/healing/
Angelou, M, 'When Great Trees Fall', *Poemhunter.com*, 2016 https://www.poemhunter.com/poem/when-great-trees-fall/

Azhar, Y; Mughal, S; Siddiqui, W J, 'Grief Reaction', *StatPearls*, 2020 *https://www.ncbi.nlm.nih.gov/books/NBK507832/#:~:text=Grief%20reactions%20 lead%20to%20complex,may%20cry%20for%20no%20reason.*

Fong, J, 'Death Cafes', *World Religions and Spirituality Project*, 2020 https:// wrldrels.org/2020/04/12/death-cafes/

Levine, S, 'Quotes', Goodreads, (n.d.) https://www.goodreads.com/quotes/183868-when-your-fear-touches-someone-s-pain-it-becomes-pity-when

Mason, J, 'Death and Its Concept', *The Philosopher's Magazine*, 2015 https:// www.philosophersmag.com/opinion/17-death-and-its-concept

Rodgers, C, 'Quotes', *Goodreads*, (n.d.) https://www.goodreads.com/author/quotes/14208796.Cristen_Rodgers

Rosenthal, M, 'Trauma Creates Change You Don't Choose', *The Minds Journal* https://themindsjournal.com/trauma-creates-change-you-dont-choose/

Rumi, 'Quotes', *Goodreads*, (n.d.) https://www.goodreads.com/quotes/7746831-be-grateful-for-your-life-every-detail-of-it-and

Rumi, 'Rumi Quotes', BrainyQuote, (n.d.) https://www.brainyquote.com/quotes/rumi_597890

Rumi, 'Rumi Quotes', BrainyQuote, (n.d.) https://www.brainyquote.com/quotes/rumi_597890

Twain, M, 'Quotes', *Goodreads*, (n.d.) https://www.goodreads.com/quotes/25647-i-do-not-fear-death-i-had-been-dead-for

ABOUT CHERISH

Cherish Editions is a bespoke self-publishing service for authors of mental health, wellbeing and inspirational books. As a division of Trigger Publishing, the UK's leading independent mental health and wellbeing publisher, we are experienced in creating and selling positive, responsible, important and inspirational books, which work to de-stigmatize the issues around mental health and improve the mental health and wellbeing of those who read our titles. Founded by Adam Shaw, a mental health advocate, author and philanthropist, and leading psychologist Lauren Callaghan, Cherish Editions aims to publish books that provide advice, support and inspiration. We nurture our authors so that their stories can unfurl on the page, helping them to share their uplifting and moving stories. Cherish Editions is unique in that a percentage of the profits from the sale of our books goes directly to leading mental health charity Shawmind, to deliver its vision to provide support for those experiencing mental ill health. Find out more about Cherish Editions by visiting:

cherisheditions.com

or by joining us on:

Twitter @cherisheditions / Facebook @cherisheditions / Instagram @cherisheditions

ABOUT SHAWMIND

A proportion of profits from the sale of all Trigger books go to their sister charity, Shawmind, also founded by Adam Shaw and Lauren Callaghan. The charity aims to ensure that everyone has access to mental health resources whenever they need them. You can find out more about the work Shawmind do by visiting their website:

shawmind.org

or joining them on:

Twitter @Shaw_Mind / Facebook @shawmindUK / Instagram @Shaw_Mind

25/09/66 - 05/09/2020